What others have said about this book:

I never knew you could eat so well, so quickly, for so cheap. With your tips I can cut my grocery bill in half! Thanks!
                              Susan C., Hermosa Beach, CA

Informative, entertaining, and best of all, this book will save me money!
                                    Kathy S., Fair Oaks, CA

I would like to have this as assigned reading for everyone between the ages of 20 and 35. They will use this all their lives.
                                DeAnn P., Citrus Heights, CA

You wouldn't think a cookbook would be so entertaining, and it's saved me money too!
                                Patty A., Citrus Heights, CA

I'm not a cook, but reading your book was fun!
                                  Fred P., Citrus Heights, CA

I was able to put this book to work right away, using only ingredients I already had on hand.
                                   Ken U., Citrus Heights, CA

I love the idea of being able to go to my cupboard and to pull out fast quick items to throw together instead of having to run to the store every time I want to cook a meal for my family.
                                    Paula S., Fair Oaks, CA

Only real life experience could have birthed this charming combination of kitchen savvy, common sense recipes, and helpful food tips. This book could help even my brother, a self-named kitchen-phobic, feed himself!
Kathy S., Davis, CA

I always joke that the guy I end up marrying will LOVE to cook – or at least like eating macaroni and cheese a lot (because it's the easiest meal for me to make!). However, after reading Suzy's book, I think that joke is history. Cooking is no longer some foreign skill only a fortunate few seem to master. I can go beyond macaroni and cheese . . . and venture into more delicious, appetizing meals. It's easier to do than I thought – plus I love the <u>variety</u> of simple recipes Suzy shares.
Catherine C., Bracebridge, Ontario, Canada

Suzy's book opened my eyes to the many creative ways I can eat interesting foods using just stuff around the house. When I'm at the grocery store now, I think of "meals per dollar,"' a concept that never even occurred to me before. I am sure that the time I invested reading the book will pay dividends for years to come!
Jim U., Arden-Arcade, CA

If you don't know how to cook, Suzy will take you by the hand and make it easy.
Cheryl M., Sacramento, CA

Too Broke to Shop and Can't Cook Anyhow!

A "How to" Guide to Frugal Cooking

By

Suzy Sharpe

Copyright © 2003, Suzy Sharpe

All Rights Reserved. No part of this book may be reproduced, stored in a retrieval system, or transmitted by any means, electronic, mechanical, photocopying, recording, or otherwise, without written permission from the author.

ISBN 1-59113-428-5

Printed in the United States of America.

For more information, contact
Sharpecooking@aol.com

Dedication

This book is dedicated to

Kenneth W. Umbach, Ph.D.

His help was more than invaluable, it was essential.

Thank you so much.

What's In This Book?

Get ready, this isn't your typical cookbook. Sit back and enjoy the ride . . .

Chapter 1.

Basic survival cooking, or:
If you have diapers and formula, it ain't an emergency.

This chapter explains how to make a variety of dinners from unlikely sources by mixing and matching anything that is sitting in your pantry and fridge. You will learn where to shop to save the most bucks, some gadgets that will make your life easier, and where to buy them really cheap!

Chapter 2.

Emergency rations, or:
How not to get into that mess in the first place.

What inexpensive things to keep on hand that will sit patiently until you need them, and won't go bad. The difference between paper economics and reality economics and how not knowing is like throwing your money out the window.

Chapter 3.

The easy bare basics of cooking, or:
Granny didn't have to measure and neither do you.

The idea that cooking is hard is a conspiracy. Cooks just want to perpetuate that idea to make themselves look good. Anything looks hard until you know the basics. This chapter will teach you the ABCs of cooking. And how to cook up a storm and not have your kitchen look like a hurricane just blew through it.

Chapter 4.

The best sauces come in a can, or:
Why Mr. Campbell is a saint.

This will show you how to camouflage those "cream of" soups to make great tasting dinners in a jiffy. No one will know you didn't make it from scratch. It will tell you how to hide those veggies so the kids won't know they're eating them.

Chapter 5.

They want me to bring WHAT! or:
There's no luck in potluck.

What you can easily make to take to a gathering that won't break the bank or embarrass you.

Chapter 6.

How to impress your company or:
If you can't do it, fake it!

You've got company coming and you don't want them to know you're a kitchen klutz. This chapter will hold your hand and show you what to make and how to dress it up so it looks like you know what you're doing.

Chapter 7.

Step by step cooking basics, or:
If you already knew how to cook, you wouldn't be reading this, would you?

You will learn the things the cookbook authors never tell you because they assume you already know: the easiest way to cook a chicken, to mash potatoes so they don't turn to mush. How to know when pasta is done. (No, you don't throw it on the wall!)

Chapter 8.

Going beyond the basics, or:
Dr. Seuss isn't so hard.

Some next steps and closing thoughts.

Foreword

Our grandmothers and great-grandmothers lived through very hard times. Many of them lived in the country. Stocking up on food for the hard winter months was a way of life for them. They grew gardens and canned vegetables and often raised their own meat. They made everything from scratch because there was no such thing as convenience foods. If you went out to eat, it was at a sit-down restaurant and it was a big deal. No take out, no drive-thrus, no boxes of Hamburger Helper® to make dinner quickly.

Then came decades of prosperity, and many forgot how to stock up for the lean times. Many don't know how to "make do" with little, and many of those are now facing a financial crisis.

We have the drive-thrus and the convenience foods, but eating there can double, or even triple your food bill. You can buy ten pounds of potatoes for the price of one small box of potatoes that will serve maybe four people.

So this book is for all of the single parents out there, for those who have lost their jobs, for the newlyweds trying to make ends meet, for anyone who is struggling financially. We can do without many things in life, but eating isn't one of them.

I hope I've helped them a little.

Suzy Sharpe

Chapter 1

Basic survival cooking, or: If you have diapers and formula it ain't an emergency.

This isn't an "eat healthy" cookbook. This isn't going to tell you 30 ways to serve tofu or how to make cute little canapés out of toast tips.

This is how to feed you and yours when you've run out of paycheck but you still have month left over. This is basic, survival cooking.

This chapter starts with what to do when there's nothing to eat in the house. Now, I'm going to say to cook the rice, or pasta, or potatoes, to boil things or simmer them. If you don't know how to do any of these things, don't worry. Chapter 7 explains how to do these and other basic things so thoroughly your baby sister could do it with her eyes closed. If you read something unfamiliar, look it up in Chapter 7.

With that said, let's get to it!

You've found yourself caught between a rock and that hard place you always hear about. You have nothing to eat, and no money to go out. The kids are banging their silverware on the table.

Don't panic! You probably have more than you think you do. What you do first is to take an inventory of everything that is edible in the place. Leave out nothing! Put down ketchup and mayo, that half bottle of salad dressing, that one potato, the can of sardines. List everything!

Now divide this list into five groups:

- <u>Starches</u>: potatoes, rice, pasta, ramen, bread, box of pancake mix, potato chips, etc.

- <u>Meat</u>: tuna, sardines, 2 pieces leftover fast-food chicken, eggs (yes, I know eggs aren't considered meat, but they're protein, put them in anyway, same with cheese), bologna, cheese, except Parmesan.

- <u>Veggies</u>: half an onion, one limp celery stalk, a bag of frozen peas, a can of mushrooms, can of stewed tomatoes.

- <u>List anything left over that isn't a condiment</u>: can of cream of chicken soup, jar of spaghetti sauce, jar of Cheese Whiz, can of tomato soup.

- <u>Everything not in another list, condiments, and spices</u>: ketchup, relish, soy sauce, mayo, salad dressing, butter, olive oil, oregano, basil, Italian seasoning (Parmesan cheese would go here).

Now, let's make some dinner!

You will mix and match something from all 5 groups. Include at least one thing from every group, if you have it. If you have a group with nothing in it, don't worry, that's OK.

If whatever is in the meat group is already cooked, great! If not already cooked, see Chapter 7.

Choose a starch and start it cooking. (Ditto the above if you don't know how.)

You will usually cut the meat into small pieces. This is how you can make those two pieces of chicken, or that tiny piece of leftover roast, or 4 slices of bologna feed four people. The more people to feed, the smaller the pieces.

> **Which spice to use where?**
>
> **Brown** spices are usually used for baking: cinnamon, nutmeg, pumpkin spice, etc.
>
> **Green** spices usually for cooking: basil, thyme, parsley, sage, oregano.
>
> **Red** spices are hot: cayenne, chili powder, paprika, but they make a good contrast if used sparingly. You know your family's "hot" comfort zone.
>
> If your green spices are brown, best not use them!
>
> When in doubt, parsley goes with anything!
>
> In this book, I'm calling anything in a can in the spices section of the store a spice. If you know the difference between herbs and spices, and you want to argue with me, why are you reading this anyway?

See what is in group #4 that you can use to make the starch slippery. Isn't the purpose of spaghetti sauce to make the spaghetti slide down easier?

For example: If you have pasta shells or potatoes, you can use that half bottle of French salad dressing, or a can of cream of chicken soup, or the can of stewed tomatoes. The stewed tomatoes would work also with rice, as will soy sauce, or cream of anything soup. Even the chunky soups could be used this way.

Then put some of the veggies together with the sauce, the starch, and the meat. I want you to realize that the variations are almost endless. Depending on what is at hand, you can mix and match from the different groups and create many different meals.

You can mix and match

- Cut up leftover chicken without the bone, stir it in with any cold pasta, salad dressing of any kind (French, Ranch, Bleu cheese, Catalina, whatever the kids will eat or whatever you like) some raw or slightly cooked veggies, and you now have world famous chicken pasta salad!

- Add soy sauce to cooked rice until it is brown all over but still dry; scramble some eggs, stir-fry that half an onion, or thaw out some frozen peas; stir fry whatever veggies are on hand. Then you have fried rice. (Stir fry is explained in Chapter 7.)

- Put potato slices in a baking pan. Over those, pour one of the "cream of" soups mixed with a can of either milk, broth, or water, and put chicken pieces on top. If the chicken is already cooked, cut it up and stir it in with it. Or put pork chops on top of peeled sliced potatoes with cream of mushroom soup. Bake for about an hour at 350 degrees while you do something else. The dish is done when you stick a fork in the potatoes and they are soft.

- Add a can of chunky soup to cooked rice, cooked pasta, or boiled cut up potatoes to stretch it to serve more people. Add some cut up cooked meat if available.

- Sauté some onions and celery (sautéing is explained in chapter 7), brown some hamburger, and add to it a couple of cans of beans (whatever beans your family likes). Spice it up with a can of chopped green chilies, or some chili powder if you have some. Go very slowly with that. You know your family's tolerance for hot stuff. Put in a little, taste it, then put in a little more if needed. You can always add more, but it's hard to take it out!

- Ramen noodles – I could write a whole chapter on ramen noodles alone! Add chopped meat and some frozen veggies to the water in a pot. That will all cook as the water heats up to boiling; then add the ramen noodles and simmer (small bubbles around the edge of the pot) for 3 minutes. You now have a very hearty soup. Add soy sauce instead of the little flavor packet that comes with the ramen noodles. Cook up two or three packages like this *with* the flavor packet but drain the water off for a main dish. You can call it Chinese spaghetti. The kids will love it, and it takes less than 10 minutes.

- There is no law that says you have to serve traditional foods at traditional times. If the only meat you have is lunch meat, cut it up in strips, heat it in a dry pan with no oil until it is a little browned and add it to the fried rice, or to ramen noodles with the water drained off, or to pasta salad.

- Make pancakes for dinner, adding cut up hot dogs or lunchmeat to the batter. The kids will love it! You can make pancakes and add slices of banana, or that can of mandarin oranges that has been sitting in the cupboard for years.

- French toast is good at any time, and it will stretch out what eggs you have. It will also use up that stale bread. French toast is explained in chapter 7.

- If the only starch you have is pancake mix, make the batter thicker than for pancakes, more like a sponge than something you can pour; spoon it over any simmering soup: chunky, "cream of," or tomato. Make sure the soup is only simmering (tiny bubbles). Cover it for about 10 minutes to make dumplings. Put leftover chicken in the soup before the pancake mix to have chicken and dumplings. Add chopped celery or frozen peas to have chicken stew with dumplings! If you are saving any milk you have for the kids' breakfast, add water or broth to the soup instead.

But you're missing one of the groups! Now what!

Let's say you don't have anything in the fourth group, nothing to make the starch slippery. You can pour yellow oil, either salad or olive oil, about 3/4ths of a cup. It doesn't matter what kind of cup, a regular coffee cup will do. Fill the rest of the cup with vinegar. Add whatever spices you have that are green, not brown. Pour them into your hand until you have a pile the size of a dime. Dump into the cup with the oil and vinegar and you now have vinegar and oil salad dressing.

Or you don't have any vinegar. Take a coffee cup, put mayo in it to about half. Add a soupspoon full of mustard. If you have brown mustard, that would be best, but if you only have yellow hot dog mustard, that will do too. Mix it together and stir it into cooked potatoes, or pasta to make a pasta or potato salad.

Now that you have the starch, the meat, and maybe some veggies, add something from the last group. Add Parmesan cheese, or parsley, or Italian seasoning. If you don't have a lot of cooking experience, just add one thing from the last group. Salt and pepper come last.

The last group is as much for appearance as for flavor. Cream of chicken soup on potatoes looks anemic until you sprinkle a little parsley on top. Now it looks like you're cooking! Dark colors on light foods and light colors (like Parmesan cheese) on dark foods.

Note: Most of the brown spices are used in baking. If you are cooking dinner, it's best not to go there. The red spices are a little hot so handle with care, thinking about your family's tastes. Most green spices are good with dinner, but use your judgment. Don't put Italian seasoning with Chinese fried rice. When in doubt, parsley – either fresh and cut up, or dried and sprinkled on – goes with anything.

Are you thinking outside of the box yet?

I will tell you in detail how to make dumplings from pancake mix, and how to scramble eggs and cook rice, everything I've mentioned here.

The purpose of this chapter has been to get you thinking about possibilities. If you're stuck with what is on hand, think about how to use what you do have instead of focusing on what you don't. Find a different way to use it.

You may find as you experiment with mixing various things, you get some combinations that don't taste good together. It isn't the end of the world.

Don't give up! Think of when you were learning to ride a bike. You took a lot of tumbles until you got the right balance. No one will die from what you made, even if the kids act like they will.

Just as you got back on that bike, get back to the kitchen. You will succeed. You can do this!

Baby powder makes a terrific, great smelling dry shampoo and cleaner. Pour it on a dry dirt spot on your carpet and rub it in. Let it set a little while, (or a day or two!) and vacuum it up.

You can use it when your cat or dog comes in covered with grease from under the car. Rub it in their coat, and brush it or blow it out with the hair dryer. If you don't get it all the first time, try it again.

Don't put it in their ears, but use it to soak up the oily medicine you put inside their ears that runs outside of their ears. Use it the same as for car grease.

Chapter 2

Emergency rations or: How not to get in that mess in the first place.

Now that the emergency is past, and you have a little money to go grocery shopping, I'm going to tell you what to buy to keep on hand for those situations. You don't have to run out and buy everything at once. Just get one or two items every time you go shopping. It doesn't hurt so much that way.

Meat group (protein).

Buy cans or packages of tuna on sale. Once in a while, a canned ham goes on sale; buy a small 1 lb. or 1-1/2 lb. one. They also have cans of chicken where you buy the tuna. Buy one or two.

> Throughout this cookbook, I will tell you to add wine. This is to camouflage the canned taste of many soups and to just make it taste good! However, if you do not want to cook with wine you can use beef or chicken broth.

There are boxes of milk that are vacuum sealed and not refrigerated. (Refrigerate after opening, though.) Buy one or two of those, or a couple of cans of evaporated milk. Those are easier to use than powdered milk, but powdered milk may be cheaper. Add the same amount of water to the evaporated milk and use it like regular milk for cooking. However, most kids are really picky about their milk and won't drink it. Don't buy condensed milk, make sure it is evaporated.

Eggs last a long time in the refrigerator – not as long as canned goods, but for weeks. If you know you are going to have a short paycheck next month buy a few dozen.

Often packages of chicken drumsticks go on sale. Buy one or two and keep them in the freezer. The family packs have 15-18 drumsticks in them. Sometimes family packs of chicken breasts come on sale. Buy a large pack, and when you get home put them in plastic bags, two to a bag, and seal them up to freeze. Then you can take out two breasts or four, or how many you may need without thawing all of them.

Buy a bag of hamburger patties or turkey burger patties and stash them in the far corner of the freezer. They don't take up much room, and you can use as much or as little as you want.

Starch group (carbohydrates).

Most starches are good to keep for a very long time. You just have to be certain to keep bugs out. Keep flour and sugar, cereals, and anything else of that sort in airtight containers or plastic bags. You don't have to buy the expensive zip lock bags. There are regular freezer bags that have twist ties and are very inexpensive.

Pasta is always good to keep on hand. Any kind of dried pasta will keep for a very long time. It doubles when it is cooked, so one cup of pasta shells makes two cups of cooked.

Beans, whatever kind your family likes, buy a pound (a small bag) and put it in something air tight.

Rice will keep virtually forever, especially if sealed. Rice triples when it is cooked, and it is very cheap, so a little goes a long way.

Bread will keep for a few months in the freezer as long as no air can get to it.

Keep a box of Bisquick or pancake mix in a sealed container. You can cut the instructions from the box and tape it or rubber band it to the container. You can usually buy Ramen noodles at about 10 cents a package. They keep for a long time and don't take up much space.

Vegetables/fruits, whatever vegetables your family likes to eat, undoubtedly come in frozen packages. Buy one and stuff it in the freezer, in the back by the turkey burgers. Buy a few cans of fruit and vegetables when they are on sale. Dried fruit is usually a little pricey. If you want to economically stock up you need to buy either canned or frozen.

Canned tomatoes – stewed, or diced, or any other kind – are very versatile. You can always use them in an emergency. They can even substitute for spaghetti sauce or extend spaghetti sauce.

For everyday cooking, however, it is good to always try to keep on hand onions and celery, if nothing else. You can cut the top third off of the celery, the part that has the leaves. Wash the cut off stalks and slice them thin. Lay them on newspaper or paper towels on a flat sheet (cookie sheet), and put them in the oven overnight. (If you live in a humid climate it may take a couple of nights.) If you have a gas oven with a pilot light, that heat will be enough to dry the celery. If you have an electric oven, or a gas oven without a pilot light, turn the oven light on and close the door. When the celery, leaves and all, is dry, put it in a jar and put on the lid. This will keep a long time in the back of your fridge, and will come in handy when money gets tight.

You can do the same to onions, but it will stink up your house. You can buy a jar of dehydrated onions at the store. Believe me, it's worth it. Dried onions can add a lot of flavor to an emergency meal. A special note to those with picky kids: you can sneak dried onions into their food where they might pick out the fresh ones. They don't notice the dried as much. Don't cook them first, just add them to the sauce. You can soak them in water if you want to, but it really isn't necessary.

Buy a small jar of chopped garlic and keep it in your fridge.

The other stuff in the pantry.

This is where you can really stock up. Buy cans of soup, especially the "cream of" soups. Cream of chicken and cream of mushroom are old standbys. The house brands are usually good, and cheaper. You are going to be adding other things to all of these, so it doesn't matter if you buy a name brand or not.

Always have a can or two of spaghetti sauce on hand; the cans cost less than the jars. You can use the turkey burger in the back corner of the freezer (the patties thaw quickly) fry it up and add the dried celery and onions if you don't have anything fresh to add to it. Dump in the spaghetti sauce, throw in some Italian seasoning, serve over whatever pasta you have on hand, and there you go! Come and get it!

Spices, herbs, and condiments.

Spices and herbs you should keep on hand, besides the dried celery and onion: Italian seasoning, dried parsley, and bay leaves (these seem expensive, but they last a long, long time).

A few recommended spices that could be useful: thyme, ground ginger, basil, oregano, and sage.

You probably have mayo, ketchup, maybe some soy sauce, a can of Parmesan cheese, or Worcestershire sauce to kick something up a little.

If you have no dressing for a salad, spoon some mayo in a small bowl, not too much, add ketchup, enough until the mayo is the color of salmon (pinkish). Stir in a small spoonful of relish, or a pickle chopped up. You have just made Thousand Island dressing!

> The best cookware you can buy is very inexpensive and is sold at the bargain stores like Wal-Mart.
>
> Buy the cookware that is stainless steel with either a copper or aluminum bottom.
>
> It cooks just as well as the black stuff that is now the fad, and will last forever!
>
> If trying to decide on whether to buy copper bottom or aluminum, both do the job. The copper is prettier, but after a few years of hard usage, either will look like they've gone through a war anyway.

Paper Economics and Reality Economics.

There is a tremendous difference between what I call "paper economics" and "reality economics."

Paper economics is what looks good on paper. You figure out what everything costs, you decide how much you have to spend, then you budget your money to get the best deal, or to spend it in the most efficient way. Sounds great doesn't it?

Reality economics is what really happens. Reality economics takes into account human nature. It takes into account things happening in a completely unexpected way. For example: When my kids were small, I went to the supermarket and diligently priced everything I needed to make their lunches to take to school. I decided the cost effectiveness of bag lunches verses buying lunch at school. I came to the conclusion bag lunches were the way to go. I would save at least $1.50/day making the lunches for my 3 kids at home. Paper economics, it looked really good. That was $7.50 a week! $30 a month! I was really getting excited! I ran out and bought two weeks worth of supplies for packing lunches.

However, I forgot one small detail. I wouldn't be around to police the "goodies" I'd bought for the sack lunches. By the third day, almost all of the lunchmeat, the fruit, the little desserts were gone.

There was no longer anything left to put into the sack lunches. I ended up giving them the money to buy their lunch at school. So, I was out not only the lunch money, but also what I'd spent on the two-week's supplies. After that rude awakening to reality economics, I just gave them the money for school lunches.

There is also the reality of if they actually eat what is packed in their lunch. If you ever worked at an elementary school at lunchtime, the trashcans are full of untouched fruit and sandwiches and everything else their doting parents packed for them.

A tip here, when the kids were older, I gave them an allowance, and that money was also for lunches at school. The deal was, if they wanted, they could pack their own lunch and keep the money. When they are in on the creation of their lunch, there is a much greater chance they will actually eat it.

Shopping tips.

Another big money waster is when you buy something out of guilt. You know to be a "good parent" you should pack some fruit in the lunch bag. You should have a well-balanced lunch in there. But think about that specific kid you're dutifully packing that fruit for. Knowing him, will he really eat it? If not, and you absolutely have to pack something healthy, at least find out what has a good trading value so instead of throwing it away he can trade it for something he likes better. You will be contributing to the good health of someone else's kid, so you get a few points for that.

Another way to waste your money is buying things on sale you don't need. You see that tomato soup is selling for six cans for two bucks! What a bargain! You snatch up six cans and bring them home. Except they sit in your pantry for years because no one in your family likes tomato soup.

That again is human nature. It is hard to pass up a bargain. In reality economics, ask yourself before you buy that sale item, "Will I really use this?" When you have that argument with yourself about whether to buy it or not, think, "If I buy those six cans of tomato soup, I will save four dollars off the regular price. But if I <u>don't</u> buy them, I will save two dollars! Either way I will save some money. What is the reality? Will I use them?"

When you are looking at the price of food, don't think price per pound. Think, "How many meals will I get for this price?" If T-bone steak is on sale for a dollar less than usual a pound, and you pick up a package of steak, think about how many meals you can get out of that package. Look over at the rib roast next to the steak. You can probably buy a whole roast for the price of the small package of steak on sale. If you buy the whole rib roast, you can cut a few steaks off of the end of it. Cut some of it into one-inch cubes and use it for stew meat or stir-fry. And you can actually use the rest of it as a roast! You can re-package the stew meat, steaks, and roast by putting them in separate freezer bags and freezing them. You can have three meals, including steak, for the price of those steaks on sale.

Plan for leftovers.

There comes a time in every family when there will never be anything left over. This is when the kids become bottomless pits. There isn't anything you can do about that. However, there are times when you can plan for leftovers.

I was fortunate enough when I was struggling, to have a freezer in my garage. Every November, when every store was enticing the holiday shoppers with sales on turkeys I would buy about six turkeys. Never all at once, of course, and usually not all at the same store, and definitely not all at the same time!

I would put those turkeys in the freezer and bring one of them out every other month. We would first eat it just as a turkey. Nothing fancy, you don't have to do all of the fixings like every day is Thanksgiving. It was more like a giant roasted chicken.

Next, I would take every scrap of meat off of the carcass (after it was cool) and put half of it back into the freezer in a freezer bag to use next week. The other half I would make into turkey enchiladas, turkey lasagna, turkey tacos. In anything you can use hamburger for, you can substitute turkey. Amazingly, my kids never got tired of eating turkey. There were so many things I could do with it.

Of course, I was fortunate enough to have a freezer. But the idea is the same. If you buy a roast, or the chicken on sale, buy it with the idea of how many meals you will get out of it. Not how much it is per pound, or per unit.

Meat will go farther if you cut it up in small pieces.

Each chicken is usually cut into eight pieces, and people will eat it by the piece, or pieces. Some will eat two or three pieces at one sitting. That chicken will probably only last one meal, with maybe one or two of the less popular pieces leftover.

If you cook the chicken, and take all of the meat off of the bone, cut it into small pieces, you can maybe get two meals out of it. Or if you buy boneless chicken you can cut it into small pieces and stretch it.

If you have two pieces of leftover chicken, those two pieces left whole could feed two people. Take the meat off of the bones, cut it up and add it to something to feed the whole family. Again, think about how many meals you will get out of the package of chicken instead of price per pound.

Where to buy your food.

There is a difference between the various kinds of supermarkets: there are the really budget mega-warehouse club stores which sell everything under the sun in bulk, the large warehouse stores with bar-bargain prices that make you unload your cart and bag your own groceries, the bargain stores that give you a club card to get a discount but they bag your groceries, and the high end supermarkets with higher prices.

> Many of the bargain stores are now advertising beef that is aged and specially selected for tenderness. They sell it with a guarantee. Wouldn't hurt to try it and see if you like it.

You can get bargains on bulk foods and other items at the mega warehouse stores, however you will almost certainly buy more things there than you intended. They can suck up your money faster than your mother's old Hoover vacuum.

You need to really be aware of reality economics. I avoid those places like the plague. However, if you really need something from one of those club stores, delegate someone else to go for you, give them the money for your item and let them take the risk of spending all their money. "Sally! You're going to Ted's Cost Less Bulk Mega Store? Could you pick up a box of those 5,000 diapers they sell there for me?"

The bargain warehouse stores and the club card stores sell the same quality of food. The warehouse stores can sell for less because of the quantity they sell and because you do the work of unloading the cart and bagging your purchases.

The bargain stores, which bag your groceries for you, can sell at lower prices because the quality of the meat and produce are slightly lower than the high-end stores. There are four main grades of meat: prime, choice, select, and standard.

The prime grade of meat usually goes to restaurants. The higher end stores carry choice and the bargain stores carry select. The difference in the grades is a matter of tenderness. The meat at both places could have come from steers grown on the same ranch, eating the same food, ending up in the same slaughterhouse. One may have less marbling (flecks of fat running through it which cause the meat to be more tender) and got stamped select. If you made a stew from a select grade of meat, it would have the same nutrition as a stew made with choice meat.

The vegetables may not be perfect in the bargain stores, maybe not as pretty. The stem may be tough, but a tomato from either store would have the same vitamins and nutrients.

The other items on sale are equal. A certain brand of beans will be identical to the same brand of beans in either store.

So, it is a question of how much money you have in your budget and what you are willing to sacrifice to stretch it.

If you are able to unload and bag your own groceries and don't mind if your vegetables are good, but not perfect, the large warehouse stores would save you the most money.

If you are picky, buy your meat and veggies from the high-end stores and everything else from one of the bargain stores. If you decide to buy everything from the bargain stores, don't feel guilty. The food will provide the necessary nutrients for your family, and the money you save will allow you to buy more of it. There are always trade offs in life. I've bought from both high-end stores and the bargain stores and often couldn't find the difference between the veggies, myself.

One of the best places to find bargains on food and cleaning supplies, among other things, is at a dollar store. There are a number of different companies springing up, but the idea is, everything in the store cost a dollar. I went there this morning and bought three loaves of bread (one for now and two to go in the freezer), a jar of chopped garlic, two large boxes of baking soda for a buck (I use it as a carpet deodorizer), a 16 oz. jar of peanut butter, and a bottle of dishwashing liquid. I saw there many different spices, rice, canned foods, spaghetti sauce, all kinds of cookies and candies, moon pies, even vitamin supplements. Go and check it out, it will be worth your time.

Brand names verses store brands.

Buy store brands of items whenever you can. Including cereals, dishwashing soaps, detergents, ice cream, frozen vegetables, anything. At least give them a try. If you can't stand any ketchup but that certain brand, buy it, but you can save a ton of money if you shy away from anything you see marketed on TV. Do you know how much it costs for one commercial? Guess who is paying for that!

I once was at a plant where they process vegetables into those square frozen packages. The end result was coming off a conveyor belt and had a lesser-known brand on the label. A few minutes later, I saw the same square packages coming off the conveyor belt with a different, house brand label on it, same green beans, same processing plant, same time of day, same machinery, different paper wrapper. Many things are like that.

Beware of Madison Avenue advertising. Those companies pay big bucks to try to find ways of selling you things you don't need, or to scare you into buying their product.

Instead of buying a mop once and using it for free for the next two years, you now need to buy a mop that has a pre-wet disposable towel on it that will not only set you back twenty bucks for the mop, but will cost you fifty cents every time you use it!

Instead of using the cutting board and washing it every time for pennies worth of soap, you need to buy disposable cutting sheets so you won't have a "germy squirmy" or whatever mess.

These companies aren't making these new products because they are concerned about your health and welfare.

People have been washing and re-using dish towels and cutting boards and mops and dusting rags for generations and the human race has survived. They want your money. If you don't have extra to spend, don't give it to them!

I loved it when they

No drawer space in your kitchen? Get a large flowerpot and put all of your large cooking utensils in it. Spoons, spatulas, whisks, everything! You can get a plain pot, or decorated, or decorate it yourself with paint.

Take a medium sized flowerpot that matches and put a plant in it (what an idea)!

Now take a matching small flowerpot and put it by the kitchen phone to hold pencils and scissors, etc.

came out with the washable disposable plates. You can re-use them! I have some of those, only I call them dishes!

Kitchen appliances, which can save you money and make your life easier, and where to buy them.

A crock-pot can make your life easier and save you money. You can cook those inexpensive cuts of meat that aren't as tender and have them tender enough to fall apart. You can dump everything into it in the morning and it's ready to eat after work

A hand blender is useful for making your own soups.

A toaster oven is more versatile than a regular slice toaster and can save you from heating up the oven and your kitchen as well.

A hand mixer for baking, making mashed potatoes, etc.

One of the appliances I use the most is an electric rice cooker. You dump the rice and the water into it, push the button, ignore it completely, and 20 minutes later it's done! You can dump in the rice, some cooked chopped meat, some broth, and those frozen veggies from the back of the freezer and when the time is up, it turns itself off! You never have to worry about it burning or overcooking.

These things are not expensive, but you can get them for very little money if you keep your eyes open at garage sales and swap meets. I bought a Braun hand blender for $1.50 and a food processor for $15. They were dirty from being in someone's garage for a while, but cleaned up really well and work just fine. Be sure though to check the appliances before you buy them: plug them in and turn them on, make sure all of the necessary parts are there.

If you are going to buy from a store, try the outlet stores, or go to the bargain stores as opposed to the high-end stores (same as for bargain and high-end groceries). Or hint around that a crock-pot is on your Christmas wish list. The one that has a pot that comes out for easy washing is best, and the bigger the better.

Chapter 3

Cooking isn't hard. That idea is a conspiracy by cooks who want to make themselves look good.

To someone who can't read, having a book tell you a story is almost magical! If you don't know how to ride a bicycle, watching someone whizzing by can even be scary!

Here are a few rules about cooking. They aren't hard at all:

- If you are inexperienced, do not leave the kitchen while you are cooking unless it's in a crock-pot, a rice cooker, or the oven.

- Always wash your hands before you start anything, wash them after you touch raw meat, wash them if you've left the kitchen, if they just feel sticky, and wash them any other time you think about it.

- Anything on the stovetop needs to be stirred once in a while. The purpose of stirring is to move the food on the bottom of the pot away from the heat so it doesn't burn. So, scrape the bottom as you stir. (I like a flat wooden spoon for this.) The thicker the food, the more you have to stir it.

- Before you start, put all the ingredients you need on the counter to make sure everything is there.

- As you use each ingredient, put it away immediately. This keeps the kitchen clean, and you will know where you left off if the phone rings or there is some other distraction. If it's still on the counter, it still needs to go in.

- Almost always cook the celery and onions first, unless stir-frying, then add the meat. The celery and onions are done when they become see-through. Garlic burns very easily so add it to the onions just before the onions are done.

- Since you can't leave the kitchen, fill the sink with hot soapy water and clean while you are waiting. When you are finished chopping everything, clean the cutting board and wipe the counter off in between stirring. When you are done, you will have dinner ready, and the only dirty dishes will be the ones you are eating off of.

- Use a different cutting board for cutting meat than you use for cutting vegetables. It doesn't matter if the board is wooden or plastic. They used to think that wooden cutting boards would harbor bacteria because they are porous, but they found out the tannic acid in the wood kills the bacteria. I would suggest the board for the meat be small enough to fit in the sink so you can wash it well.

- Butter burns the quickest, if cooking with it keep the heat low. Olive oil can take more heat, but burns if the heat is higher than medium. Use peanut or canola oil for high heat. If whatever you are using starts smoking and turns brown immediately lift the pan off the stove and turn the heat down. Put the pan back on if it has cooled a little. If it is smoking a lot and smells, you will have to clean the pan and start over.

- If a pan catches on fire, DO NOT PUT WATER ON IT! Slap a lid on it to smother the flames. If the burner is on fire, dump a lot of baking soda on it to smother the flames.

- Don't add salt to the food until it is done cooking. If you add the salt and the liquid evaporates it will then be too salty. The exception is in the water for boiling pasta.

- Wine will make any dairy product curdle; so don't add milk to the pot until the wine has evaporated.

- For safety reasons never put a knife (or any other) blade in water where you can't see it. Always leave it on the counter until you are ready to wash it.

Most cooking has certain steps you take usually in the same order every time.

This order will work in almost any cooking you are doing except stir-frying. That will be covered in, you guessed it, chapter 7!

1. Assemble all ingredients.

2. Chop everything that needs to be chopped, starting with the vegetables (you can fudge a bit on this when you have some experience and can do two or more things at once, but in the beginning it's best to just get everything cut up first).

3. Turn the burner on, then pour the oil, (or put the butter, or whatever you are going to use) in the pan. Pour a little puddle in the center of the pan about the diameter of the top of a soda can. Put the burner on medium heat.

4. When it is hot, add the onions and celery to the pan and stir until they are transparent.

5. Add more oil if needed, then the meat. Make sure the oil is hot before you add the meat; you want it to sizzle and to sear the outside so the juices won't flow out and it will stay moist. Never use a fork to turn the meat, it will pierce it and the juices will run out.

6. When there is a brown crust on the bottom (brown but *not* black), add enough wine to cover the bottom of the pan – just about a quarter of an inch. You want it all to evaporate so don't put too much. This is called deglazing. Scrape all of the brown off the bottom and let it dissolve into the wine, it has all of the flavor and will make it taste wonderful!

7. Add any liquid you are going to use: a can of soup with milk or water or broth, depending on what you are making; or a can of spaghetti sauce; or just some broth without the soup; maybe more wine.

8. After the liquid has started simmering (little bubbles around the edge of the pot), add potatoes or other veggies and let it cook. Do not let it boil hard, meaning large bubbles. This will make any meat really tough, and it is in more danger of burning (you didn't forget to stir it did you)? Turn the heat down if the bubbles are large and rapid.

9. You can feel when the veggies or the potatoes are done when you stick a fork into them and it goes in easily. Green veggies will turn a darker green, if they turn olive green they have been cooking too long. Artichokes are the exception.

10. Last, you might want to thicken the sauce, depending on what you are cooking. Some sauces

will need it, some won't. Put cornstarch in a small bowl or a coffee cup. Maybe a quarter of a cup, it depends on how much you are making. You can always add more later, so you should be conservative. Add a very small amount of water and stir it with your fingers or a fork, making sure all lumps are out. Add enough water to make it pourable.

11. Use a whisk or a spoon, but the whisk is better, and stir the sauce continuously as you pour the cornstarch slurry (that's what it's called) into the sauce. In a little while the sauce will become thicker. If you add too much at once, the sauce will get really thick fast, just add more of whatever liquid you put in already.

Your dinner should now be done.

To clean a wire whisk:

Swish it in the soapy dishwater like you're trying to scramble some eggs . . . the whisk will be completely clean and you won't have to wipe each wire.

Chapter 4

The best sauces come in a can, or Mr. Campbell is a saint.

You can make any "cream of" soup easily taste like a million bucks.

<u>Chicken or mushroom sauce</u>

- Chop up some onions and celery. About 1 quarter of an onion per person, and one half a celery stalk per person (if you are cooking for children, the smaller the pieces, the better).

- Pour olive oil, or canola oil in the bottom of a large pan, enough to make a puddle the size of the top of a soda can. Turn on the heat, medium.

> There is a little product you can buy in the packaged sauces/gravy section called "Kitchen Bouquet." This is a little bottle of a dark liquid that will keep for <u>years</u> in your cupboard. It adds a little flavor to any sauce/gravy you are making, but its real purpose is to make it dark. You don't want to serve a roast with mushroom sauce that is white – eewww! Not very appetizing. Stir in a few drops of this stuff and it will be a lovely brown color.

- Add the onions and celery in the pot and stir until they are transparent. Put in a little garlic if you want. This is where you add chopped mushrooms if you want them. The mushrooms will add some liquid to the pot. Cook until the liquid has evaporated.

- Now, when it is dry and turning brown, pour white wine into the pot, just covering the bottom. Don't put too much as you will want it to evaporate. You need to stay right there and watch it because once the liquid is gone what remains will burn quickly.

- When it has evaporated, turn the heat down and add a can or two of "cream of" soup. How many depends on how many are going to eat.

- To every can of soup, add half a can of broth.

- Parsley flakes will be good to add here, or other spices. Now is also the time to add salt and pepper. Serve the sauce with whatever you want.

Cheese sauce

- Pour a little wine in the bottom of a pot. White or red, depends on how strong a flavor you want it to have. Red is stronger than white.

- When it is almost evaporated, add the cream of cheese soup and either a can of broth, or half a can depending on how thick you want the sauce to be. Cook until heated through.

Spaghetti sauce

- In a large pot, put your onions and celery and enough oil to make a small puddle the size of soda can top. (When you have a thick sauce like this, you can add chopped, peeled zucchini. Without the peel, it turns to mush and disappears, making the sauce even thicker and fooling the kids into eating some veggies.)

- Add whatever meat you are going to put in, hamburger, leftover turkey, etc. If it is cooked first go onto the next step, if it is raw, sear the meat until it is brown.

- Add mushrooms and cook until the liquid from the mushrooms is evaporated and there is a brown crust on the bottom.

- Immediately pour in a little wine to coat the bottom of the pot, not too much!

- When the wine has evaporated, add the can or two of spaghetti sauce and some Italian Seasoning. I would add a small pile the size of a nickel

> The wine is what helps to take the canned taste away from the soups. Since it is evaporated, there is ultimately no alcohol in the sauce itself, only the taste of the wine. Just as in drinking wine, use white for light colored meat, and red for dark meat. If you don't want to use wine, you can substitute either chicken or beef broth.

for every can of sauce I put in. You can experiment with your family's tastes. Heat it through and serve it over pasta.

Chapter 5

They want me to bring WHAT! or: There's no luck in potluck.

You've been invited to a gathering by one of those super efficient hosts and people are assigned dishes by the initial of their last name! You can't get away with bringing chips or your standby 2-liter bottles of some soft drink.

Let's say you're still pretty lucky and have to bring a salad. What you bring depends on what time of year it is. A fruit salad would be cheaper in the summer, as would a melon salad. A green salad in the spring, as lettuce and other greens are cheaper then. In the winter, a pasta salad or potato salad will do.

When making any kind of salad think color. You want at least three different colors.

For a fruit salad:

Use at least three colors of fruit. Make one of them grapes that you've pulled off the stems, and cut the rest of the fruit into different shapes. You will need to peel most kinds of fruit first. Cut Kiwi in round slices, it looks pretty that way. Round fruits should be in crescents, like orange segments. (Take as much of the white part of the orange off as you can, as it can be bitter.)

Cut the green leafy part off of strawberries and cut the big ones in half. (Use either a bunch of grapes, or big beautiful whole strawberries with the green leaves still on as a decoration.

Avoid bananas and avocados as they tend to turn brown unless dipped in lemon juice, and they get mushy. If you use apples, you will need to dip them in lemon juice so they will stay white.

> **To clean a solid head of lettuce:**
>
> Hold the head in both hands with the stem pointing down. Tap the stem on the counter then twist it. It will come out. Pull the head apart with your fingers and rinse in water. Turn it over and drain the water out. Too much water on the lettuce when you store it will turn it that icky rusty color.

You can add a bottle of mango Snapple, or a can of limeade frozen concentrate thawed but with no water added, but it isn't absolutely necessary. These can also be added to the melon salad. Either of these will give the fruit or melon salads a little kick.

For a melon salad:

Three colors of melon: red watermelon, orange cantaloupe, and green seedless grapes; or watermelon, some green melon and purple seedless grapes; strawberries, cantaloupe, and green grapes. You won't need a lot of anything, and the secret is to make certain there are no seeds in anything. That means, either to pick out the watermelon seeds, use only the center, or buy seedless.

Cut everything into pieces of the same size, meaning grape sized. To do this cut the cantaloupe in half lengthwise so the halves look oblong instead of round. Scoop the seeds out with a spoon, or use your hands (You did already wash your hands, right?) Cut crescents out of the halves about an inch wide. Make cuts the width of each crescent down to the rind. Finally, take a thin knife and cut the pieces off of the rind.

Wash the grapes and pull them off of the stem. Make sure you throw away any that look "funny" or are gross. Save a small bunch on the stem with maybe 5 or 6 grapes still on it. This will go on top as a decoration.

For a green salad:

Use leafy lettuce, not the compact ball kind (iceberg lettuce). Thinking three colors, buy one green head, one that is reddish, and at least one vegetable of a different color. You can buy a red/purple cabbage, or some cherry tomatoes, or grate some carrots.

Wash the lettuce and make sure all of the excess water is drained off. Some people dry it, but that isn't necessary if it is going to be eaten right away. Too much water makes the lettuce turn brown and icky, but that shouldn't be a problem in this case. You don't want excess water diluting the dressing though.

Tear or cut the lettuce into little bite-sized pieces. Then add any tomatoes, or carrots, or cabbage, whatever you decided to put in it.

Buy a bottle of salad dressing of some kind, pour it into a bowl to be spooned out, or leave it in the bottle. You can buy one at the dollar store, or make your own if you are REALLY brave. Thousand Island dressing is on page 19, and oil & vinegar on page 11.

Pasta and potato salads:

These are covered in Chapter 7. You can bring one of these as a salad, or if you got stuck with a side dish.

You've been asked to bring a side dish

Side dishes are the most flexible. You can bring a pasta or potato salad, or any of the starch dishes: scalloped potatoes, pot of beans, or some vegetables.

A **vegetable tray** would do as a side dish, or as an appetizer, sometimes called finger food. You should have at least five different vegetables, preferably of different colors. All of the vegetables should be cut into large pieces to make them easier to eat with the fingers.

Buy a cucumber, peel it, run a fork down the sides lengthwise, and slice it into circles. The circles will have cute ridges on the edges. Cut celery on a diagonal, cauliflower and broccoli into small flowers, zucchini diagonally into oblong pieces. Buy cherry tomatoes and baby carrots, and two green peppers. Cut the tops off of both green peppers and clean out any seeds. One of the green peppers you need whole, and the other cut into slices.

Buy a jar of ranch dressing, or ranch flavored sour cream, or flavored cream cheese and spoon it into the green pepper you didn't slice up. Stick a spoon in it. Then put it last into whatever you are arranging the vegetables on.

Arrange the different groups of vegetables into a basket, or a bowl, or on a tray, whatever is handy.

I used to bring a veggie tray for about 150 people in a punch bowl. Making it myself, it cost less than $20.

Deviled eggs:

Put the eggs into a pot, size depending on how many you are cooking. Fill the pot with cold water, covering the eggs. Put the burner on high heat until the water is boiling hard (lots of big bubbles). Once you notice the water is finally boiling, turn off the heat, but leave the pot sitting on the burner. Set a timer for 30 minutes. After 30 minutes, take the pot to the sink and pour out the hot water. Run cold water into the pot cooling the eggs as fast as you can. This keeps the eggs from getting that gray color around the yellow part.

Take the shell off the eggs, trying not to destroy them. Some will fall apart, or have too much shell stick to them, use those in the potato salad, or in an egg salad, or just eat them right there. Cut the eggs in half lengthwise and put the yolk into a bowl. Put the white part on whatever plate you are going to serve them on.

Smash the yolks with a fork, mashing them up really good. Add enough mayo to equal about a quarter of the volume of the yolks. Then add a regular cereal spoon of brown mustard, or the yellow hot dog mustard if that's all you have. Stir it up until it's smooth. Taste the mixture to see if it has a little "kick" from the mustard. If you have a lot of eggs, you may need to add more mustard.

You will need a Ziploc bag for this next part, as a sandwich bag isn't strong enough. Now, spoon the yolk mixture into the Ziploc bag. Seal it up getting as much air out of the bag as possible. Snip off a bottom corner of the bag with scissors. Make sure it is a very small hole left, no larger than a pea.

Hold the opening over the depression in each egg white and squeeze the bag gently. The yolk mixture should come out like it is tiny soft serve ice cream.

Move the bag as you are squeezing as if you are filling a tiny ice cream cone. Sprinkle a little paprika on the eggs for contrast, not too much, it is for appearance only. Then, if you want to get fancy, add a tiny sprig of dill to each egg, or slice a pickle like matchsticks and put one on each egg, or a leaf of lemon balm, or a small mint leaf. If you don't have enough to put on every egg, place whatever you are placing randomly. You just want something green for contrast.

Worst case, you have to bring an entree

You're a big time loser in the potluck lottery and have to bring an entree, which usually means some kind of meat. Here's what you can do.

Bar-b-que chicken wings:

Buy a 5-pound bag of chicken party wings and a bottle of bar-b-que sauce: any brand, any flavor, whatever is cheapest. Pour the sauce into a bowl. There is no need to thaw the wings, but separate them into individual pieces.

Dip each piece into the bowl and cover with the sauce, and then lay it on a flat, cookie sheet. You may need two sheets for 5 pounds of wings.

Bake them at 350 degrees. After one hour, take one of the drumettes and taste it. It should pull easily away from the bone. If it doesn't, bake it for 10 minutes more, checking it again.

Note: There is a paper called parchment paper that is used for baking. Put a sheet of that paper on the baking sheet before you put the wings on it. It will save you a lot of clean up time.

Tortellini in wine sauce:

Buy a bag of frozen tortellini, if it is stuffed with meat, it is an entree; if it is stuffed with cheese it is a side dish. (Isn't that easy?)

You will cook it according to the regular pasta directions, except it is done when it floats to the top. Before you cook the tortellini, start the water boiling while you work on the sauce.

If the tortellini is stuffed with cheese or chicken, use cream of chicken soup and chicken broth. If the tortellini is beef, use cream of mushroom soup and beef broth. The directions for the wine sauce are in chapter 4.

A crock-pot is a good thing to transport hot food in, even if you didn't cook it in the crock-pot. And you can keep it hot if dinner isn't served right away.

Dessert is the easiest

Ice cream wouldn't work very well at a potluck, and this book doesn't cover baking, so you will just have to buy something. What you buy would depend on how much money you have, a bag of cookies, a cake, or some pie. If you spend a lot of money on an ice cream mousse cake, leave it in the box. If you bought cheap sugar cookies, put them in a fancy bowl. Those little animal cookies that are coated with pink and white icing are usually really popular, and no one will mind you only spent two bucks.

Brie and Baguette:

If you don't feel right bringing a bag of cookies you can buy a whole little round or a wedge-shaped slice of Brie cheese. You can get one for usually five bucks if you don't go to a deli. Take the wrapper off and no one will know it's not that expensive imported stuff.

Buy a baguette of bread; this is a really skinny loaf like a loaf of French bread. Slice it on a diagonal, so the slices are oblong, not round.

If you have a cutting board that looks good, put the Brie on this, maybe putting something green near it or under it like lettuce, or parsley, or a sprig of dill. If your cutting boards look like they came through a war put the Brie on a plate. If the board/plate is big enough, arrange the bread around it, or put it into a separate basket. Put a nice looking knife next to the cheese. It doesn't have to be a sharp knife; a butter knife will do.

If you bought a round of Brie, cut out a wedge-shaped slice and place it next to the round to get it started or no one will touch it. People can be funny sometimes. The idea is, people cut some cheese off and smear it on the bread.

Chapter 6

How to impress your company, or: If you can't do it, at least you can fake it!

Say you can't afford a set of fine china for dinner, but you like having people over and like to dress things up. If you can't afford having everything match, and you didn't inherit Grandmama's china, have <u>nothing</u> match. Start checking out the garage sales and thrift stores.

Buy a place setting each of different patterns. Buy a soup tureen of an entirely different pattern. You can limit yourself to only patterns of one color, say all pink, or go all out and buy every hue. You can buy only patterns of flowers and set the table with a whole garden. Or don't even buy china, buy all white stoneware in various styles, or a different color, or all different colors.

The same with glasses; buy wine glasses of various styles, then it won't be a catastrophe if one gets broken. Buy silverware of various styles also. When you set the table, either have every place setting matching within itself, or have nothing matching at that place setting. Make certain every piece of silverware does not match any other piece at that setting.

The point is to make it look deliberate. You don't want to have four places matching and then two others on the everyday plates. You can pull it off if you have confidence!

Of course, you may only have everyday plates. In that case, distract the guest's eyes away from the place settings by having something spectacular as a centerpiece, or a beautiful lace tablecloth. You can buy tablecloth material at any fabric store. Measure how much you need and just hem the ends. Some of it is beautiful and inexpensive.

Have candles everywhere, they will attract the eye. Put a real flower on everyone's plate and flowers around the table. If you've picked them from your (or someone else's) garden, make certain you have washed all the bugs off!

For the menu, serve things you are comfortable with. Don't serve something you have never made before unless you are really brave. If you want something special that's good, just make it the week before so you won't have any last minute surprises – something like a dress rehearsal. Now, this will be a dress rehearsal, not the real thing. Don't make something a week before and save it for the party! You'll have to make it again!

You can punch anything up and make it seem special by naming it. In chapter 4, I told you how to make a wine sauce from the "cream of" soups. When you serve it to your company, call it by the type of wine: Chicken Tortellini in Chardonnay Sauce, or Beef in Burgundy Sauce. Call the roasted chicken Grandma's Roasted Chicken, and the store bought apple pie is now Mom's Apple Pie.

For a classy, easy dessert, buy vanilla ice cream and dish it out into wine glasses before your guests arrive. Stick some kind of cookie in it, an Oreo, a Fiddle Flake, or one of those fancy cookies. Put them all back in the freezer. Just before you serve the dessert, heat some caramel sauce, or fudge sauce (from the store, of course!) in the microwave and spoon it over the ice cream. Serve it immediately! To make it even more special, add a <u>tiny</u> bit of Triple Sec, or Grand Marnier, or Amaretto to the sauce as you are heating it.

Suggested menu ideas:

Do the mix and match again, except the five groups should be: appetizer, meat, starch, vegetable, and dessert.

> Garlic burns easily. Put it in just before the onions are done.

The "how to cook it" is in the next chapter.

Appetizers:

Their purpose is to take the edge off of your guests' hunger and give them something to do so they won't complain if dinner is a little late.

You can serve either:

- Brie and baguette
- A vegetable tray
- Bar-B-Que Chicken wings (if it won't clash with the other meat)
- Chips and a dip. This you can buy ready-made. Depending on how fancy you want to get, serve it in a fancy bowl.

Butter and Oil

Butter burns quickly but it has a good flavor -- low to medium heat

Olive Oil is more healthy, and many people love the taste. It has a higher burn temperature than butter -- medium heat

Salad, peanut, or canola oil has the highest burn temperature, use it for frying foods -- high heat

Starches:

This is to fill people up so they don't eat so much expensive meat!

- Rice Pilaf
- Twice-baked potatoes
- Pasta with wine sauce
- Scalloped potatoes

Meat:

In many people's eyes the only reason to come to dinner.

- Roast with some kind of wine sauce
- Baked chicken quarters, or bar-b-que chicken quarters, or chicken quarters cordon bleu.
- Stuffed Cornish game hens (this is if you <u>really</u> want to get fancy – even my mother could make this, and that's saying <u>a lot)</u>!

Vegetables:

Usually not fancy in themselves, but you can spiff them up some. I would stay away from frozen or canned for a special occasion.

- Artichokes with parsley butter

- Corn on the cob

- Mixed farm-fresh vegetables (remember what I said about naming things?) whatever is in season: carrots and broccoli and cauliflower, or corn and lima beans and red bell peppers. Again, think three colors. The vegetables should be the same size so they will cook at the same time.

- Broccoli or cauliflower in a cheese sauce. However, you should only have one sauce in the menu. If you are serving baked chicken quarters, have veggies in cheese sauce, but if you are spooning a sauce over the baked chicken (that looks really fancy), serve the veggies with butter.

Dessert:

- Re-read the dessert section on potlucks. It's best here to just buy a cake or a pie and serve it with ice cream, or do the cookies and ice cream in a wine glass.

- Heat up some canned fruit like peaches or Mandarin oranges, drain most of the syrup and spike them with a <u>tiny</u> bit of a flavored liqueur. Use your judgment; booze with a licorice flavor probably wouldn't taste too good with peaches, etc. Amaretto and cooked apples taste great! Serve it over the ice cream in the wine glasses.

- Put the store bought cake or pie on a pretty dish. If the cake is dark, sprinkle powdered sugar over the plate first. If the cake is light, sprinkle cocoa powder. Use some kind of wire strainer to get it uniform and non-lumpy. Put it in the strainer, hold it over the plate, and tap it once lightly on the side. Do it again until the whole plate is uniform. Or put a paper doily down on the plate, sprinkle the powdered sugar or cocoa powder and lift the doily off – very easy and very impressive. If you don't have any baking cocoa powder, use the sugared stuff you use to make chocolate milk for the kids. If no powdered sugar, use regular sugar, but not too much, and the doily trick won't work as well.

- Spiff your dessert up with some fresh fruit on top or on the plate, a small bunch of grapes, dip apple slices in lemon juice (so they won't turn brown) and put on that apple pie, whole strawberries on something chocolate.

- You could do the Brie and baguette, but some people don't consider cheese to be a dessert so it depends on your company.

The most important thing to remember when you are entertaining is that you will set the mood of the party. If you are nervous and stressed out, trying to have everything perfect, your guests will be nervous and stressed out. If you are calm and relaxed, they will be too.

Music is very important. If you want a jumping party, play jumping music. If your intention is a relaxed calm party, play calm, relaxing music. If the music is good, you can serve chips and dip in an empty warehouse and the party will be a great one!

The best way to throw a party with little money is to make it a potluck! Have everybody bring something, I usually let them choose either: something to drink, or some finger food, or just themselves. I will put out a veggie basket and Brie and baguette, maybe some chicken wings (see potluck chapter).

Inviting people over is a great way to get wine for free. Even if dinner isn't a potluck, many will bring a bottle of wine. I rarely buy wine. When I do, I go to a local dollar store. Everything sold there costs a dollar and they usually have both red and white wine. It doesn't have to be the best wine, as I'm going to use it for cooking.

Here is a good time to talk about an old story about stone soup. It seems a vagabond came to a poor village. Asking for something to eat, he was told there wasn't enough for him.

He started a fire in the town square and put on a large pot of water. In the pot, he put some stones, being careful to choose the "right ones" and making an exhibition of washing them. The curious villagers asked him what he was doing.

"Making stone soup," was the answer.

"There is no such thing!" the villagers answered.

The vagabond just sipped his stone broth and smiled, "It's wonderful, the only thing it needs is maybe a little onion."

"I have an onion!" a woman cried and ran to get it. To make a long story short, whenever the vagabond tasted his soup and said it needed something, the one of the villagers brought it, vegetables and spices and even a little meat.

By the time it was done, the stone soup fed the whole village. This is something that should be remembered when you have little money. If everyone contributes a little, the results can be great.

Once a large group of friends of mine went on an outing to play in the snow (being a California Cutie, the only time I see snow is when I want to go and play in it).

After a while, everyone was getting tired and hungry. Someone suggested we all go to a local restaurant. I didn't have any money to feed myself, and my three kids at that restaurant.

I looked at a friend of mine who was also a single Mom and saw the same thing in her eyes. I said, "I have a better idea! Let's everybody come over to my house for spaghetti! I have some sauce and the pasta!"

Someone else said they could bring some garlic bread, a couple of other people brought the makings for a salad, and some others stopped at the store and bought some soda.

We had much more fun than we would have had at any restaurant.

Chapter 7

Step by step cooking basics or: If you already knew how to cook, you wouldn't be reading this, would you?

Methods

Bake: cooking with dry heat in the oven. It refers to bakery goods, vegetables, and fish. Most things are baked at 350 degrees, so if you aren't sure what temperature to use, that is a good guess.

Braise: usually means cooking meat in a small amount of liquid after searing it. You don't want it sitting in too much liquid as it will make the meat tough. However, the liquid it is cooking in will make a great sauce. This is an excellent way to make a tough cut of meat fork tender.

You can do this on top of the stove, as in a pot roast, inside the oven, or in a crock-pot. Often potatoes and other vegetables are added to lift the meat out of the juices and it makes the whole meal in one pot. The liquid can be water, wine, broth, beer, or just about anything. You need to cover it to keep the steam in.

Boil: large bubbles coming up all over the pot. You must be careful to stir so that nothing burns. Never boil meat as it will make it tough. If you don't want the pot to boil, you have to turn the heat down to make it simmer.

If you are reading a recipe, and it says a hard boil or a rolling boil, it means the contents of the pot look like down the cone of an erupting volcano.

Deglaze: adding a small amount of liquid (usually wine) to a pan to dissolve the cooking residue. This gives it flavor and as an added bonus, the pan will be easier to clean.

Roast: cooking with dry heat in the oven and it usually refers to meats and poultry. You do not cover the meat when it is roasting. Usually meat is put on a rack of some kind to lift it out of the juices and it allows hot air to circulate.

Sear: cooking meat on a very high heat in a canola or peanut oil. You want to seal the outside so the juices will stay in and make it moist. High heat, hot oil, be careful! It is sometimes called browning, as that is what happens to meat when you sear it.

> Oh oh! Dropped a piece of the eggshell in the scrambled eggs while cracking them? Use another piece of the shell to "scoop" it out. The raw eggs will part like the Red Sea.

Simmer: when little bubbles come up on the edge of what is in the pot. You still have to be careful that it doesn't burn. This is good for most stovetop cooking.

Steam: cooking with steam. The steam can come from added water, as in a small amount of water in a covered pot with vegetables or from the food itself. Baked potatoes which are wrapped in foil are really steamed as they cook in the steam trapped in the potato (see how to cook potatoes).

You can steam vegetables in an oven-proof container with a lid and a little bit of water, or wrapped in foil with a little bit of water. There are pots and gadgets called steamers that lift the vegetables out of the water.

Stir-fry: cooking something quickly over high heat. Many use a wok to do this. However, the best Chinese cook I know, who came over on the boat, used a giant cast iron skillet.

1. Put a little peanut or canola oil in a pan and turn the burner on high. If the oil gets too hot while you are cooking, and starts to smoke, you can add a little more to cool it off. You can also lift the pan off of the burner to cool it down a bit. NEVER LEAVE A PAN ALONE if you have it on high heat. Do not use olive oil as it burns easily.

2. Dump the different items in, one kind at a time, whether a vegetable, or chopped meat, and constantly move them around until done. Cook the white vegetables first so the chlorophyll from the green vegetables won't turn them yellow.

3. Put each vegetable into a bowl after it is done, add a little more oil to the pan if needed and cook the next vegetable, adding it to the same bowl. White vegetables are done when they are transparent. They should be cooked first, as the green vegetables will turn them yellow. Green vegetables are done when they are dark green. Stir-fried vegetables should be crisp, not limp. If you want to add garlic, put it in with the onions when the onions are almost done, garlic burns very quickly. If you have large pieces of vegetables, for example broccoli, you can add a little water and cover the pan with a lid. This speeds things up a bit, but you still can't leave the pan.

4. Cook any mushrooms last as they have lots of liquid in them, and they will turn anything else cooked in the pan brown.

5. Now add any meat you are going to cook. If it is already cooked, you will only need to heat it up, but if it isn't cooked, cut it into small pieces, about one inch on a side, it will cook quickly anyway. Stir-fry the meat: chicken until it has turned white, other meat until it has turned brown.

6. Now deglaze it. This means to add a small amount of liquid to the pan, usually some kind of alcoholic beverage, but you can use broth or even water. Just be careful! (You cannot deglaze with milk though, as it will burn in the high heat.) The liquid will immediately start boiling as it hits the

pan and create a lot of steam. This is good! Sake is wonderful to deglaze with in stir-frying, but white or red wine or whatever you have on hand will work. Scrape all of the residue from the veggies and the meat off of the bottom of the pan as you deglaze it. This is where the flavor is.

7. When most of the liquid has evaporated, you can add soy sauce, or a combination of half soy sauce/half oyster sauce, or a store bought teriyaki sauce. How much depends on how much you now have in the bowl. This shouldn't start boiling immediately as you were using a little liquid to deglaze, and you should be using more in this step.

8. When the concoction in the pan starts to simmer, you can add cornstarch slurry to thicken it, if you want.

9. Pour it all in the bowl and stir to coat everything in there.

You can stir-fry any vegetables, except maybe artichokes. I would recommend onions cut large, celery cut on a diagonal, sliced water chestnuts, broccoli in little flowerettes, green pepper sliced in strips, those flat Chinese pea pods, and bean sprouts.

Scramble a few eggs in a separate pan (or they will be brown—ugh), make a lot of sauce in step #7, and add the eggs and the sauce to cooked rice. You now have **fried rice**.

Most of the time spent here will be in cutting up the food. You must have everything ready to cook before you turn on the burner because you will have no time after that. It goes so fast and is so hot; I don't recommend you leave it for an instant.

Sauté: Sautéing means to cook something, (usually vegetables) over a medium heat in some kind of oil or grease until they are transparent or limp. You should stir them often so they cook evenly and do not burn. You will do this constantly when you start to cook the onions and celery in most recipes.

Thicken: with a cornstarch and water mix. There are other ways to thicken things, but this is the easiest. Put some cornstarch in a cup, about ¼ of whatever cup you are using. Add enough water to make it thin and pourable, this is called slurry.

When whatever you are trying to thicken starts simmering, pour the slurry into the pan, stirring constantly. Don't stop stirring until it has thickened enough and is ready to serve. If it doesn't get thick enough, add more slurry. If it gets too thick, add more of whatever liquid you put in it. (See Kitchen Bouquet at the end of chapter 4.)

How to cook starches

Beans: most beans need to be soaked overnight in water. Run water over them as you check for rocks or other foreign material. Put them in the pot you are going to cook them in and add water until it is 3 or 4 inches over the beans. They will expand and it is better to have too much water than too little. The next morning, or 6 hours later, pour out the water and rinse the beans. This is important as it will help get rid of the gas. Add water again covering the beans and add any vegetables you want to put in them, like onions and celery.

If you have a crock pot great! Turn it on high (I don't have a lot of patience, and beans are hard to overcook) put on the lid and go to work. If not, put it on the burner, turn it on medium and stick around until it comes to a boil. When it does, turn it to very low, cover it and stick pretty close where you check on it throughout the day. Or put it in the oven, turn it to about 250 degrees and stay nearby, but you don't have to worry about it. Cook it all day. The beans are done when they are soft. Usually, the longer you cook them, the better they are.

Dumplings: There are two kinds of dumplings, dropped and rolled. Open a can of biscuits and place them on some simmering liquid, cover the pot and cook for 10 minutes. Turn the heat low, because you can't stir them. You can tell your Grandma on the phone you are making rolled dumplings. They were rolled out at the factory, right? Cut them up in quarters if you want to, and when she says she doesn't believe you, you can tell her you're just now cutting them out!

For dropped dumplings, pour either Bisquick or pancake mix in a cereal bowl. Don't fill it completely, leave some room to stir it. Now add enough water to make a dough. It should look like a sponge instead of something you can pour. Scoop out a forkful and scrape the fork off on the side of the pot with the simmering whatever-you-are-cooking in it, letting it drop onto the liquid. Keep doing this, dropping it in different places in the pot until it is all gone from the bowl. Cover the pot for 10 minutes, keeping the heat low so it doesn't burn. The pancake mix dumplings are really sweet and can be addicting. The kids may eat these even if they think dumplings are gross. Call them cake dumplings.

> NEVER put any blade in dishwater where you cannot see it! That is a great way to get cut!
>
> Keep dirty blades on the counter until you wash them.
>
> That goes for knives, blender blades, food processor blades, or anything else sharp!

Pasta: Put a big pot of water on the stove and turn it on high. Add some salt, about a one second pour from the round salt container. You can't really put in too much, or too little. The salt makes the water boil at a different temperature and it will all be drained off. Some people add oil to the pot, enough to make an oil slick the size of the top of a can of soda. The oil will help keep it from boiling over, out of the pot. When the water is boiling hard (lots of big bubbles) put in the pasta. Stir it as you put it in, and stir it once in a while as you are cooking it to make it separate.

How long you cook it depends on how big the pieces are. Something small will cook for maybe 5 minutes, whereas spaghetti will cook for maybe 8 minutes. The package will tell you how long for each type of pasta. Keep the water boiling during this time.

When the time is close, fish out a piece and bite into it. It will be firm all the way through, but not mushy. This is called *al dente*. If you bite into it and it feels tough in the center, it needs to cook a little more. Keep testing it.

When it is done, strain the water out using something with holes. There are various utensils, colanders, strainers, special pots that with holes that you lift out. Jack Lemmon used a tennis racket in his movie, *The Apartment*. The idea is to just get the water out. Some people rinse it with hot water afterwards, some don't. If you are going to immediately cover it with some kind of sauce, it isn't necessary to put anything on the pasta. However, if it is going to sit around in a bowl by itself for a while, you may want to stir a little butter in it so it won't stick together.

For **Ramen noodles** however, get the water boiling and put the brick of noodles into it. Turn the burner off, and leave it for 3 minutes only. They will be done.

Potatoes: When **baking** a potato, scrub it first to get any grit off (ugh!) paying attention to the "eyes," those indented places. Either prick it with a fork a few times on top, or slice it with a knife, not deeply. This allows some of the steam to come out. Put them in the oven and bake them for about an hour. They can bake at different temperatures from 250 degrees for two hours or so, to 450 for 45 minutes to an hour. This is great because they can bake along with just about anything else that is baking in there. Reach in with a pot holder and give them a little squeeze. The potatoes that are done will feel soft.

Here, you are going to say, "Uhn, uhnn, you have to wrap them in foil first." Not so, I don't know who started that, but those aren't baked potatoes. Restaurants may have started doing that because it might keep them hot longer when they are serving a kazillion of them and can't bake them fresh all night. People saw the restaurants doing it and thought it was the "proper way." Those potatoes are not baked. They cook in their own steam. If you bake two potatoes, one with foil, one without, you will see their texture is very different. The one without the foil will be fluffy and dry, the one with will be more "solid" and heavy. (See "Twice Baked Potatoes" in the recipes below.)

To **boil potatoes**, you can wash them first and boil them with the skin on, or peel them. If you boil them with the skins on, the skin will be hot when you are trying to peel it off. If you peel them, cut them up, size depending on what you want to do with them. Usually try to get things that are cooking together of similar size, both for appearance and to have them finish cooking at the same time. If you are cutting potatoes to put in a corn chowder, cut them very small; if for a pot roast, cut them into quarters. If you need them done in a hurry, cut them into small pieces. As you are peeling them and cutting them up, unless you are actually working on the potato, you have to keep them covered in water or they will turn brown from the air. Cook them at a hard boil for 20 minutes to 30 or so. They are done when you push a fork in one and it is soft all the way through.

Scalloped potatoes are done in the oven. Peel and slice them, it really doesn't matter too much how thick or thin you cut them. Thin is fancy for company, thick saves time for dinner. Put them in a casserole dish or a cake pan and cover with a can of cream of soup mixed with ½ can of milk, and a pinch of parsley. Bake them for about an hour, at 350, unless you have a lot of potatoes in the pan and it's thick. Then it may need some more time.

Add grated cheddar cheese to the soup before you pour it over the potatoes for **Potatoes au Gratin.** There should be more soup than cheese in the mixture.

When the potatoes are done you can **mash** them. Don't let the cooked potatoes sit in the water. If you can't get to them right away, drain the water off. As the water turns cold, the potatoes will absorb it and will be soupy. This is probably the most common mistake in making mashed potatoes. There are different ways to mash them, depending on what utensils you have, and how fanatical you are about lumps. To have them completely lump free: there is a gadget that is shaped like a big can, with small holes in the bottom of it. You put the potatoes in this, and push them through the bottom. This is called ricing them. Next, use a mixer which may leave a few lumps, and last, you can use a potato "masher" which has a grill or wire on the bottom and you push it through the potatoes. This leaves the most lumps but will build your muscles.

Now that you have the potatoes mashed up, heat some milk and butter in a pan, or the microwave. Maybe a fourth of a cup of milk and a pat of butter for each potato you put in the pot. When it is hot, (careful, it will burn easily and the pan will be a horror to clean) add it very slowly to the potatoes as you whip them, either with a whisk, a spoon, or a mixer. Do it slowly because how much you add depends a lot on how much water the potatoes have absorbed. Keep adding the milk and mix until the potatoes are fluffy and moist looking. You can now add some salt and pepper: pour each into your palm and when you have a mound the size of a nickel, dump it in and mix it up. This much would be for a large bowl of potatoes. That part depends on your family's tastes.

I'm scared to tell you how to **fry potatoes**. I have visions of houses burning down and lawsuits. I affirm that I am not responsible for anything stupid you may do while trying out the instructions in this book. (Review how to put out a pan and burner fire in chapter 3 ----DO NOT PUT WATER ON A FIRE ON THE STOVE!!)

Peel the potatoes, cut them in the style of **French Fries** you like and keep them in water until you are ready to fry them. The really thin kind like at the Mac place take a lot of time and effort to cut, so make them in strips the diameter of a dime. You can call them "Old Fashioned French Fries." Heat about an inch of canola or peanut oil in a pan. Turn it on high. Drain the potatoes and towel them dry. When the oil is good and hot, but not smoking (do not leave it for anything!!) put enough of them in the pan to cover the bottom, but they are still covered by the oil. If you put them in the oil with water on them, the water will start the oil spitting and will get really nasty. I'm talking burns and blisters on your arms here. When done, the fries if large will become transparent and then start browning, if they are small they will turn golden brown. Lift them out and drain them on a paper towel.

If you can work fast, you can cut the potatoes as you are frying others and not have to put them in the water in the first place. Many people don't even peel the potatoes first, just scrub them (remember the grit – ugh!). If you can avoid the whole water thing, the better.

There is a handy appliance you can find at many garage sales and that is a small fryer with various names. It is usually black and about the size of a small loaf of bread turned on its end. If you see one of the deep cookers that hold a gallon or two of oil pass it by. If you could use that thing, you wouldn't be reading this book. But the little fry babies came in handy of you fry a lot of potatoes for your family, and you can keep the used oil in it.

A fire on the stove whether in a pan or on the burner is burning either grease or oil. If you throw water on it, the burning oil or grease will splash out and you will then have a large kitchen fire instead of a small stove one.

Put a lid on it!

If the burner is on fire, dump baking soda on it to smother the flames.

Either grate the potatoes, or cut them in small cubes to make **hash browns.** If you work quickly, you can avoid the putting in water thing. Pour a small amount of oil in the bottom of a pan, just barely coating the bottom and turn the heat almost all the way high, maybe halfway between medium and high on the knob. Put enough potatoes in the pan to cover the bottom, but not deep. Leave it alone! As the potatoes cook, unless you have it too high, they will sit there and get a nice crust on the bottom. This is the "browns" in the hash browns. If you stir it, it will never turn brown. If you cover it, it will steam instead of fry and will never get brown. Just watch it! Use the flat spatula to pick up a corner and peek under. You can see when they are brown, and it should come up in one piece, more or less. Turn it over like it's a giant pancake. Cook it a little longer to get the potatoes which were on the very top of the pancake done. Don't wait for this side to brown, just check to see if they are transparent. Put it on some paper towels, add a little more oil to the pan if needed, and do the next batch. You need to stay and make sure the "pancake" doesn't burn. Add chopped or grated onions and green peppers to make "**Country fries."**

Rice: Rice triples when it is cooked, so one cup of uncooked will give you three cups of cooked rice. The ratio of water to rice is 2:1 (two measures of water to one of rice). So if you fill a coffee cup with rice, dump it in the pot and add two coffee cups of water. Put in a little bit of salt, how much depending on how much rice you are cooking. If you aren't used to cooking, it is best to be conservative, or don't add any at all.

Turn the burner on high and stay close. When it is boiling, turn it low until the water is only simmering. Put a cover on the pot and set a timer for 20 minutes. Many experienced cooks have an internal clock which tells them when something is done, but a timer is a really good investment that will save you money in not throwing out burned food. All of the water should be gone and the rice tender when it is done.

For rice **pilaf,** use broth instead of water. Sauté some chopped onion and green peppers or celery and add it to the pot before you cook the rice.

For **Spanish rice**, sauté some chopped onion and green pepper and add to the dry rice in the pot. Add tomato juice or V-8 juice for half of the water.

How to Cook Meat

See the section on stir-frying to see how **to stir-fry any meat**. The procedure is the same for all. You can cut it into strips, or into cubes. It makes no difference.

Beef: You can **roast** beef in the oven, on the stove top, or in a crock-pot. It is easy to know what to buy in the store, as it will be called a roast.

Anything next to a rib or bone on the steer or on the loin will be more tender and flavorful than other cuts, so look for those names. If you buy a large roast, you can often cut some not bad steaks off of it if it is a rib roast or a loin. Meat that is roasted is cooked relatively dry. It is good to lift it up somehow to keep it from the juices. You can use a rack, or vegetables like potatoes and carrots (they won't disintegrate) and put the roast on top of them.

Unless it is roasted in the oven, it is good to sear the meat first.

Chicken: For a **whole chicken**, make sure it is thawed. Reach in the large cavity and pull out all the stuff in there. Don't worry about doing anything with it, just throw it away, or give it to the cat or something. Some people wash the chicken first, and some think it washes away the flavor. That isn't that important.

Fold the wings as if the chicken were putting them behind its head. You can salt and pepper the inside, or not. You can stuff the cavity with stuffing or rice, or not. If you stuff it, it will take a little longer to cook, and you will want the temperature to be lower,

(325 degrees) so the wings and legs won't get too done while waiting for the rest of the chicken.

Put it in a baking pan on some kind of a rack, or chopped vegetables. Or you can just put it in the pan, a chicken doesn't have all that much juice in it. Bake it for an hour. At 350 degrees.

To see if it is done, look at the drumstick. The meat should be pulling away from the bone. If it has cooked for an hour and the meat isn't pulling away, cook it for 10 minutes more and check it again. This is the easiest way to cook chicken. This method of testing for doneness works whenever you are cooking drumsticks in any way. And if the drumstick is done, the rest of the chicken will be too.

To bake **chicken parts**, it is usually best to find something to coat them with, such as bar-b-que sauce, or bread crumbs. Taking the skin off or leaving it on is entirely up to you. I know people who think leaving the skin on is akin to eating boiled lizard entrails, and others who think the skin is the best part. If you want it skinless, use a paper towel to grip the skin, it's easier that way.

Pour whatever you are using for coating into a bowl. You can use bar-b-que sauce, brush it with soy sauce, coat it with bread crumbs, crushed corn flakes, just about anything. It's not necessary to buy that shake stuff. If you like it, buy some poultry seasoning or seasoning salt and mix it with a little flour.

If you are using dry ingredients, you can put it into a plastic bag instead of the bowl. Do not re-use whatever is in the bowl that has had raw chicken in it. I know it is tempting to brush that left-over bar-b-que sauce on it, but you're flirting with salmonella poisoning.

Dip the chicken pieces in the bowl or shake in the bag and lay them out on a cookie sheet. If you put a sheet of parchment paper (bought on a roll like foil in the baggie/foil department of some stores) the clean up will be minimal. Have them close together, but not touching.

Bake them for an hour at 350 degrees. See above about checking for doneness. If you aren't cooking any drumsticks, you can cut into a meaty piece to make sure it isn't pink inside.

To make **smothered chicken**, you will need to de-skin the chicken pieces. The skin cooked in any liquid gets spongy and gross. Lay the pieces in a casserole dish (that's a dish with sides), or use a cake pan.

Mix some "cream of" soup with ¾'s can of water and ¼ can of white wine, or one whole can of milk. You can even liven it up more by sautéing some onions and celery and adding them to the soup.

Pour this over the chicken in the pan, cover it with foil or something, and bake for about an hour and a half, again, the magic 350 degrees. This is good served with rice or noodles as it makes a kind of "gravy."

You can slice up some potatoes, pour the soup on top of them, put the chicken on top of all of that, and still bake it for the same amount of time.

Eggs: To cook **hard boiled** eggs, put them in a pot and cover them with an inch of cold water. Put a little salt in the water, a pile about the size of half a dime. Put them on high heat, and when it is on a rolling boil, turn the heat off and set the timer for 30 minutes. When the timer goes off, immediately pour out the hot water and pour in cold water. Let the cold water run in the pan for a little while, until the eggs are cool.

To **fry** eggs, it's easiest to use a non-stick pan. Put a tiny bit of butter, bacon grease, cooking spray, something to make the pan a little slippery. The heat should be medium to low. Crack the egg on the side of the pan, and gently open it up, pouring the egg into the pan. If you get some eggshell in there, use another piece of eggshell to fish it out.

Sunny-side-up, you don't flip it over, the white should be done and not transparent still, but people who like it this way aren't picky about that, or they would order their eggs, over easy. It should freely move about the pan as you tilt it.

Over easy is when the white is cooked enough to freely move around the pan as you tilt it, turn the egg over. Don't rush this process. Your heat should be on the medium to low side, or it will turn brown and the white won't be done. You can cut into the egg next to the yolk to see if the white is done. People who like their eggs this way like the whole white to be done and the yolk still runny.

Over hard is the same as over easy except you break the yolk to make sure it is done all the way through.

To **scramble** eggs, break how many you want into a bowl, fishing out any shell that falls in by using another piece of shell. Stir them up until it all is yellow. You can add a little milk to stretch them, if you want, but not so much they become white and not yellow.

Again, put something in the pan to make it slippery, some kind of grease/spray and pour the mixed-up eggs in there. The heat should always be medium to low when cooking any kind of fried eggs.

Stir the eggs a little bit, and slowly. You need to let them have time to harden before you stir them more. Stop when the eggs are almost completely dry. They will continue to cook after you take them out of the pan. There should be no liquid remaining, but they should be moist, not dry. Add salt and pepper.

Omelets are scrambled eggs that aren't stirred. Pour the egg mix into a pan, just like scrambled. Top it with meat or cheese or veggies, whatever you like on your omelets. Make sure the heat is low!

A nice little trick is to cover the pan with something. A heat-proof plate will do. Leave it there for a little while, until the omelet slides around easily, and the top looks dry. You can fold it over once, or into thirds, or not at all.

If the bottom gets a crust on it and gets too brown, the heat is too high.

French toast is bread dipped in scrambled eggs. Thick sliced bread is best, but you can use just about any kind of bread you want.

Put a piece of bread into the bowl with the eggs and turn it over to coat both sides. Leave it in until the bread has soaked enough to pick up the eggs, but you don't want it dissolving.

Cook it on a grill, or in that same pan with the slippery stuff.

Again, low & slow is the key. The toast is done when it looks dry, and if you cut into it, it is dry. You will need to practice a little bit to get it right. A lot depends on how much you soak the bread.

Lunchmeat: Most lunchmeat has a lot of fat in it, so you don't have to add anything to make it slippery.

Cut it into whatever shape you want, if cooking a whole slice, you will need to cut the edges so it will lay flat and not curl, or cut it in half. Turn the burner on medium and let it get brown. It will shrink a little. If in strips, stir it, if not, turn it over to brown the other side. You will need to drain it on paper towels, and it wouldn't hurt to blot the top with towels too.

Pork: Cooking the various cuts of pork is very much like cooking beef. It will turn white inside when it is done.

Pork chops or steaks can be baked in the oven, on top of scalloped potatoes.

Bacon: The secret to cooking bacon on top of the stove is to keep the heat real low. If it spits at you, it is too high. Turn it when the fat is no longer transparent. Then remove it before the fat part turns dark brown.

How to Cook Vegetables

Artichokes: Cut off the top fourth of the artichoke, the stem flush with the base, and take scissors and cut off the tips of the leaves. Fill the pot about one inch high with water. The fancy chefs will tie a slice of lemon to the top and bottom, but you can just pour a shot or two of lemon juice in the water. This will keep it from discoloring, and flavor it a little. Steam the chokes for about 45 minutes. They will be olive green when done, and the leaves will pull off easily.

Kids usually like to eat these, as you pull off the leaves, and scrape the meat off the base of the leaves with your teeth. You can dip them in melted butter, melted butter with green herbs (especially parsley if you want to look fancy) or mayo, ranch dressing, etc. When all the leaves are gone, scrape the fuzzy stuff off of the heart and eat the whole thing.

Corn: To cook corn on the cob, get a lot of water boiling. Put about one second's worth of salt from the round salt container in the water. Clean the ears by pulling the green leaves off and the hairlike silk. Put them in the pot for only 5 minutes. It will be tender. If you cook it longer the corn will be tough.

Broccoli: Cut the individual "flowers" off of the stalk. If you like, you can peel the stalk and use more of the broccoli. If it isn't peeled, it often can be tough. Just take your knife and cut a little into the bark, hold onto the cut part with your thumb and pull it off. You can stir-fry or steam it. Sprinkle grated cheese (any kind) on it when it is done to look and taste special.

Cauliflower: Cut off any parts of the cauliflower that are brown, cut the "flowerettes" off of the stem. Steam it. You can also sprinkle it with grated cheese.

Frozen: For almost all frozen vegetables, you can put them in a microwave bowl and nuke them for 5 minutes. There's no need to cover them or add water. Or put them in a pot, add about an inch of water and steam them. They get done quickly once the water starts boiling.

Fresh: Most vegetables are good if steamed. Put vegetables that are cut pretty much the same size in a pot with an inch of water. How long they cook depends on how big they are. The green vegetables are done when they turn dark green. Add some grated cheese over them if you like. Most vegetables can be stir-fried.

Peas: The best peas are frozen. You can add them to the water of anything you are cooking. Put them in the water for ramen noodles and they will cook by the time the water is boiling. Put them in with the macaroni when you make macaroni and cheese. Or just put them in a little microwave dish and nuke them for 5 minutes.

Zucchini: Zucchini is a magical vegetable. It will disappear if the peel isn't around to keep it together. This is great to know to sneak some vegetables into kids who won't touch anything green. You can peel it and add it to anything with a thick sauce like spaghetti sauce or chili. Otherwise, keep the peel on it and steam it, stir-fry, grill it, or bake it. It cooks very quickly. I like to cut it thick and grill it on my little grill. Then I put whatever grated cheese I have handy on it.

Sauces: Sauces are covered in Chapter 4.

Various Recipes

Garlic Bread: Take a loaf of French bread and cut diagonal slices in it, but not all of the way through. Let some butter sit out to soften it, or soften it in the microwave. Stir up some garlic powder, or chopped garlic from that jar in the fridge. It is better if you can make the garlic butter ahead of time so the flavor gets to permeate the butter. How much to put in depends on how much you like garlic. It is best to be conservative at first. Try one quarter of a teaspoon to one stick of butter at first. You can always increase the garlic next time.

Slather it in each diagonal slice in the loaf. Wrap it in foil and bake in the oven for about 20 minutes. Then unwrap it and bake it 10 minutes more.

Fancy Artichokes: The same as the artichokes mentioned above, except cut them in half lengthwise and remove the fuzzy part before cooking. They will cook in a little less time. You can fill the "hole" on top of the heart with mayo, or flavored butter, whatever you want. Be creative!

Cornish Game Hens Stuffed with Rice: To really impress someone, figure on one whole game hen per person. Get a box of one of the brands of rice with wild rice and cook it according to package directions, or make rice pilaf. Stuff the cooked rice into the large cavity after preparing it like the roasting chicken above. Roast in the oven for an hour, just like miniature chickens.

Chinese Stir-Fry: Read carefully the instructions on stir-frying under cooking methods in this chapter. Stir-fry in this order: onions, sliced water chestnuts (canned), bean sprouts, Chinese pea pods, celery cut on a diagonal, green peppers cut in strips, and any other vegetable you like to eat. My kids were especially fond of broccoli, but you do have to peel the stems.

Now stir-fry mushrooms if you want some in, and last, whatever type of meat you are going to include. If the meat is cooked already, just heat it up, but if it is raw, stir-fry it until it is done and it changes color. Deglaze with wine or sake.

Mix together half soy sauce and half oyster sauce (bought by the bottle in the Chinese food section) to the meat and heat that up. How much depends on how much you are making and how much rice you want to put the sauce on.

To make **chow mein**: cook ramen or straight Chinese noodles according to directions (usually 3 minutes in boiling water). Drain them. Put a little oil in the bottom of the wok or skillet, and I mean a little, just enough to coat it. Take just enough cooked noodles to put one layer on the bottom of the pan. When they are stiff and brown, pick it up and turn it over for a few seconds. Then add it to a large bowl with paper towels to soak up the excess oil. Add a little more oil and repeat this until all of the noodles are cooked. Then take the paper towels out of the bowl, and continue as in cooking Chinese stir-fry. Add each ingredient one at a time to the same bowl.

Baked Chicken Quarters Cordon Bleu: The drumstick and the thigh still connected together make up chicken quarters. When having company, figure on one per person.

Cut a slit along each side of the bone in the thigh and drumstick. Don't cut all of the way through, and make the cut on the top so the melted cheese won't run out.

Put a slice of ham, cut thin as for lunchmeat, on top of a thin slice of Swiss cheese and cut them together into slices one-quarter-inch thick. Insert one of these combined slices of ham and cheese into each slit in the chicken leg and thigh.

Pour seasoned bread crumbs (you can buy a can at the store) into a bowl and pat each quarter with the crumbs. Make sure the whole piece is covered.

Place each piece cut side up on a cookie sheet and bake it for an hour. They are done when the meat pulls away from the bone on the drumstick.

Deviled Eggs: See Chapter 5.

Twice Baked Potatoes: Cook potatoes as instructed under baked potatoes. Do not cover with foil. After they are done, cut one inch off of the top of each one. Use a spoon to scoop out the insides. Mash what came from the inside in a bowl. Add a little butter, milk, and grated Cheddar cheese. Spoon it back into the empty potato skin heaping it over. Put them on a flat cookie sheet and put back in a 350 degree over for 15 to 30 minutes. They will be done when the top is browned a little.

Pasta Salad: There are as many different recipes for pasta and potato salad as there are families. This would be a good time to try following a recipe that you find for this. You know the basics now.

However, if you don't have a recipe to try, cook up some pasta, the shape doesn't matter, except spaghetti is harder to deal with.

Cut onions and celery up fine and sauté them. Some people add black olive slices, or hard boiled eggs. If you add more vegetables, sauté them with the onions, and cut them the same size so they will cook the same.

This can include carrots, peas, beans (just add them straight from the can!) If you remember your Mom used to add different stuff, go for it! Be creative!

> To cut up an avocado, cut it in half lengthwise and remove the seed. Holding one half in your hand, take the tip of a knife and cut the "meat" to the peel, either in slices or squares. Take a large spoon and scoop the meat out of the peel.

Add this to cooked, cold pasta.

Now, put some mayo in a cereal bowl, and add mustard to it. A good ratio is two large heaping spoons of mustard to a cereal bowl of mayo. Mix it all up!

Potato Salad: Pretty much the same as pasta salad, only substitute cooked potatoes for the pasta. Cut the potatoes into bite sized pieces.

Chapter 8

Going beyond the basics, or Dr. Seuss isn't so hard.

I remember when in 8th grade home economics class I had to sew a skirt.

There were a lot of girls in that class who already made their own clothes and knew all the tricks and the procedures, and names of things. Unfortunately, I was not one of them. We didn't have a sewing machine, and my mother wouldn't have known what to do with one if we'd had.

These girls always got a big smile from the teacher when they brought in the second or third article of clothing they had made that week. I didn't even know where to go to buy the material. Fortunately, I had a couple of girlfriends who took pity on my ignorance of things sewing, and who helped me as best they could.

So, with a little pride, I finally turned in my skirt. I'd put in a zipper and everything, and thought it was pretty great, a little green mini skirt.

My teacher literally threw it in my face and told me, "You get an 'F,' you didn't pink the seams!"

I was flabbergasted. I didn't even know what that meant! I wasn't even sure what a seam was! Of course, I understand all of that now. It seems so simple.

That is how cooking is. If you don't know the terminology, don't have a lot of experience, it can be a daunting task. Maybe you can get someone to show you to how to fix one or two "specialties." You learn how to make a mean macaroni and cheese, and if it comes in a box with instructions, you can do it. But recipes seem to be written in a foreign language. You feel like "real cooking" is way beyond your abilities.

Not so.

Think about when you were first learning to read. You sounded out the words and took all afternoon to read *The Cat in the Hat*. After reading through it three or four times, you could speed through it as fast as your tongue would allow you to go.

You graduated on to other books and with each one it got a little easier. Finally, you could pick up *It Happened One Morning on Mulberry Street* and you whizzed through it on the first try.

Dr. Seuss didn't get easier, you practiced and gained confidence. You got better!

If you follow what I've written in this book, if you practice it, you will have the necessary "alphabet" to cook anything you want to. You know the basics, the words. You know how to put them together. You will have some setbacks, you didn't get every word right at first either. But you should have more edible dinners than non-edible ones.

Then, when you decide to experiment and make *coq au vin*, you read through a few recipes to see what's actually in *coq au vin,* and you say, "Geeze, it's just like smothered chicken, only they deglaze it with red wine and use shallots instead of onions! Piece of cake!"

Once you have the basics, you can do anything. As you gain experience, it will get not only easier and easier, but you will start to understand things. "This recipe says to simmer this, that's so the meat won't get tough."

You will actually be a <u>better</u> cook than many others because you won't be enslaved to a specific recipe. You will be able to decide that even though this cookbook says to put this herb in, "My kids don't like that, so I'm going to put in this other one." You will be able to experiment and feel freedom!

So be creative in your cooking! Don't be afraid – fear destroys creativity.

Here's to a lifetime of great cooking!

> *Suzy Sharpe has been a single Mom for 17 years. She attended LederWolff Culinary Academy in Sacramento, California. Her hobbies include dancing, gardening, writing, throwing large parties, reading, and did I mention dancing?*
>
> **Contact Suzy at Sharpecooking@aol.com**

Be one of the first to buy my sequel: *Cooking Outside the Box*

It will tell you how to easily duplicate those expensive boxed dinners for just pennies!

Send me your email address and I will tell you when and where to get it.

All addresses will be strictly confidential and used <u>only</u> to tell you when the book is out. I promise!

NOTES

NOTES

Printed in the United States
54108LVS00001B/74